Seasons
of
Singleness

RHUNDA ARMSTEAD

Fulton Books
Meadville, PA

Published by Fulton Books 2023

ISBN 979-8-88731-767-0 (paperback)
ISBN 979-8-88731-768-7 (digital)

Printed in the United States of America

Contents

Introduction

I have often heard being single described as a season in life that will pass over time. To imply this implies that singleness occurs as a pattern of events that come and go based on an allotted set of time, a season. Having been single all my adult life, I began to challenge that theory. Seasons come, and seasons go, but this place and space in my life seem to have taken root with no foreseen end. When it does change, I don't want it to reoccur and come back as seasons do. I believe that singleness is more than a season and extended durations of singleness will invoke several states of emotions that repeatedly cycle over periods of time, which are seasons. Consequently, I've learned to prepare for the seasons of singleness the same way that I prepare for climate and culture seasons.

Oymyakon, Russia, approximately two hundred miles from the Arctic Circle, has the lowest recorded temperature of -90 degrees and is deemed to be the coldest inhabited place on earth. The average temperature during winter months is -58 degrees, which directly affects food security, building infrastructure, and clothing costs. Natives have learned to adapt to the frigid freezing winters by embracing the excessive costs of clothing (especially coats) and surviving with limited options of meat and fresh vegetation whereas visitors often struggle for even short stays and find it unimaginable to live there. Residents of coastal cities that are prone to flooding due to hurricanes build their homes on stakes several feet above the ground in preparation for high water that may fill their land. Football fanatics prepare relentlessly for their season of beer, food, tailgates, and parties to celebrate victories of their favorite football team.

These examples demonstrate the true definition and key characteristics of a season. First, seasons are reoccurring without a known end to the recurrence. Second, seasons are predictive and start times are usually defined. Third, seasons only last for a specified amount of time. Based on my personal experience, this does not describe singleness, and its characteristics do not match the key characteristics of a season. While in my place of singleness, I've found myself going through several cycles that are recurring and predictive and last for allotted periods of time. These are the seasons of singleness! As with any other season, I must prepare, adapt, and adjust for the seasons that I encounter while in my place of singleness.

Season of Transition

ransitions refer to the release of existing patterns, thoughts, behaviors, or locations in preparation of a forthcoming circumstance. This release may be self-initiated originating from an internal desire or a response to an unforeseen and uncontrollable shift in circumstances. Regardless of the reason for transition, transitions are often found to be difficult because of required actions to release the known in pursuit of the unknown. Entering into the region of singleness comes with many faces and a variety of emotions. There's the college grad who is finally living on their own and excited to enter singleness with high hopes of only staying temporarily. Then there's the divorcee who may be broken from a failed marriage and never planned to be in this place of singleness. It may be the widow/widower who never thought that they'd have to learn to live without their spouse but have found themselves single. Singles enter into singleness many different ways, but the adjustments are the same, which is to learn how to live and enjoy the journey instead of carrying it as a plaque of punishment. It's important to realize that God allows sudden shifts in our circumstances to push transition and progression. God wants His children to become better, excel more, do more, and become everything that He has designed and created them to become. God wants His people to be a witness to His power and might and to become a demonstrated statue of reference for others to see His power at work.

When I graduated from college, I stayed close to home and had a host of friends, family, and colleagues around me. I was comfortable in my familiar setting and my geographic location. However, I could not find gainful employment that utilized acquired skillsets or met financial needs to sustain rent, car payment, student loan payments, and basic necessities. As a result, I moved across the country to a city where I had no friends and very little (but close) family. The culture was very different from how I grew up, and it sent my heart into spiritual cardiac arrest. I absolutely hated it! The people were weird, bougie, and selfish, and the climate was cold and freezing! I grew up in a warm climate, and I was suddenly thrust into an environment of long durations of subzero temperatures and several feet of snow each winter. This was not a welcomed transition!

Not long ago, a very close family member passed away due to a horrific attack of cancer throughout her body. I talked to her weekly for hours at a time, and she was available whenever I wanted to talk regardless of the time of day or night. Whenever I couldn't sleep, I would call her, and she would talk to me until I was ready to fall asleep, and she always kept me company via telephone when I had to drive significant distances by myself. Her passing was truly heartbreaking, and to see her body suffer and break down the way that it did was an even worse truth to endure. This was not a welcomed transition!

Two of my closest friends passed away literally months apart. One of my friends drove trucks and would *always* show up or call during my lowest moments. Whenever I felt alone and by myself, this guy would pop up with a big smile on his face as happy as could be. It was like God himself was saying, "See, I'm right here!" That friend is no longer here on earth, and again he was inflicted with illness that broke down his body and soon after took his life.

Life can throw very powerful and unexpected blows. However, the blows are not to harm, but are to strengthen and to prepare us for greater things to come. During a hurricane, palm trees are thrust to the ground during the heavy winds and rain, but after the storm, the sun shines, and the palm trees spring back up. The storms did not weaken the tree, but the forceful hits caused the trees' roots to dig deeper, which ultimately made the tree stronger. I've learned that when various storms and transitions come into my life, God wants me to act like the palm tree and dig deeper (rooted in His word) and ultimately become stronger! I've heard it said that God does not always test our faith, but he tests our character to prepare us for the next level he wants to take us to. When I'm being pushed down by the winds of life, just as the palm tree rises stronger when the sun shines, I will rise stronger when the *s-o-n* rises in my life. That's the exciting point made in James 1:2 when it says, "Count it all joy when you fall into divers' temptation." We know that God promises not to harm us and to give us an expected end (Jeremiah 29:11), and promotion is just on the other side of the test.

I have learned that life does not always grant the mapped plan that I've prepared for myself, but my faith and pursuit of God will lead me to places of purpose and destiny. By moving to the city that I did not want to move to, I was blessed beyond what I ever thought I could have. God blessed me with gainful employment and broke struggles and strongholds that might not have been broken staying surrounded by the same friends and associates that I had before. God used me as a vessel to lead several teenage girls and a few adults into a relationship with Christ. This is what is meant by the scripture, "The steps of a good man are ordered by the Lord" (Psalm 27:23). I never wanted to live far from my hometown and never in a northern state, but my ways are not his ways, and my thoughts are not his thought (Isaiah 55:9). God knows what's best for me, and I have learned to enter transitions with peace knowing that what's on the other side is better than what I've seen in my past (Haggai 2:9).

My friends and loved ones who passed *are* now healed! They are no longer suffering, and their lives have impacted me as well as the lives of many others. My friend who showed up on occasion is still a reminder of God's nearness to me, and I know God is still saying, "See, I'm right here!" I've learned that God is a sustainer (Psalm 55:2). My aunt, the close relative who passed, has taught me the value of life and to never take the simple and everyday blessings that God has given us for granted. According to the physicians caring for her, she should have been dead almost two years prior to her death, which taught me the value of perseverance and endurance, and I saw the true faithfulness of God in that situation (1 Corinthians 1:9). He didn't have to allow her that extra time with family, but we asked for the time, and He gave it. I learned that "the Lord is nigh to the broken heart" (Psalm 34:18), and I thank God continually for every season and every situation that He's used to build my character and to mold me into the person that he would have for me to be.

Season of Loneliness

I believe loneliness is a state of mind that magnifies empty spaces and ignores present moments. It poses a continuous belief of emptiness by personifying itself as a permanent state. It often births anxiety and fear, which seeks fulfillment by latching onto the first person encountered with hopes of removing fear, doubt, and neglect. It often ignores burdens of proof to false love and challenges the sincerity of pure love that stands before it. Nonetheless, the emotional presence of loneliness is only a season. As with any other season, its occurrence cannot necessarily be stopped, but it can be successfully conquered with the necessary preparation.

It's during seasons of loneliness when emotional vulnerability is high, and the wrong person will almost always appear. It's during my loneliest seasons that the absolute worse person for me will surface and tell me all the things that I want to hear. When emotions are high, it's very easy to latch on to unhealthy relationships as the thought of having somebody begins to feel better than the reality of being alone. This is an open door that the enemy uses as an entrance to infiltrate my heart and emotions, which controls my thoughts and emotions, which ultimately controls my life. Because of this, I've learned not to entertain unhealthy relationships at all! Don't get me wrong. The attempt to satisfy temporary emotional voids is enormously strong during this season. Over time, I've learned to stop and think about the cost of a bad relationship. It will cost my peace, integrity, and self-esteem and potentially hinder the God-ordained purpose for my life. The stakes are high, and it's not worth the cost. Once the *excitement* of the new relationship passes, I would then be faced with loneliness plus paying the costs of having been in a toxic relationship. I have learned to allow God to lead my life and to trust Him through the process. God created me and can fill any void that I have in my life, including loneliness.

It was challenging to perceive being alone without feeling lonely. The truth is, having *somebody* in my life has never removed loneliness or filled internal voids. It brings happiness, a temporary satisfaction based on circumstances, but as soon as the *circumstances* of the relationship change, loneliness is there with more strength and resilience than when it first surfaced. I've discovered that the source of loneliness is not the absence of another person, but it is the absence of internal peace and contentment. This is the reason why many of my married friends confess that they feel lonely at times. The existence of loneliness is not contingent upon anyone else but self, which means I am the only person who can change my feelings of loneliness. So I must prepare for its arrival.

The first and most important preparation that I made was to establish a relationship with God through Christ. This is by far the most imperative form of preparation needed to conquer loneliness. Romans 8:31 states, "If God be for us, who can be against us?" The same force and power that raised Jesus from the dead is the same power that lives in me and has made me more than a conqueror (Romans 8:37) even against the forces of loneliness.

My next step of preparation was understanding my triggers for loneliness. Loneliness is not always present, so I started paying attention to situations that precede my feelings of loneliness. For me, a recent relationship change, passing of a relative or close friend, and health or financial challenges usually precede my season of loneliness. Becoming aware of my triggers affords me the opportunity to mentally prepare for the lonely season and the attacks that are soon coming my way. It is during these times that I began to increase my prayer time, start planning my next trip, schedule time to meet with friends, and look for fun and exciting activities to participate in. For me, not spending a lot of time alone during one these transitions help me to conquer the season.

Another important preparation for me has been the evaluation of associations. Emotional sensitivities are habitually strengthened through wrong associations. These are people who have had failed relationships and enjoy seeing my relationship fail. These are people who have financial struggles and love to see me struggle financially. They somehow believe that my bad situation justifies the dysfunctions of their continuous bad choices and outcomes of their life. These are the people who say things like "There are no good men" and "Everybody is broke." These are the people that I do my best to avoid while going through lonely seasons. I seek to be around people who are progressive, uplifting, and inspiring.

I also like to find books that focus on the specific situation that triggered my season of loneliness. This not only brings hope to my situation, but it also gives strategies and tools to implement. Of course, whenever I start implementing strategies and using tools to change my situation, there is always a distraction from someone who will attack my focus in some way. I'm then reminded of the story of Nehemiah when he started to rebuild the wall of Jerusalem that was broke down and destroyed by fire (Nehemiah 1:3). People began to mock him and speak negativity over his task of rebuilding the wall, but he continued his task (Nehemiah 4). Once the enemies started seeing progress, they became angry and united to stop the work of rebuilding the wall, but God strengthened Nehemiah and his followers, and they were able to complete their assignment, and the wall was rebuilt (Nehemiah 4). My wall has been broken relationships, job loss, and loss of family members and friends, just to name a few. When they were destroyed, no one came against me, but when I started to rebuild, it seemed as though everything and everybody came against me. Just as God strengthened Nehemiah, He strengthened me to continue to move forward and not negate the tasks that I started to complete. The more I moved forward, the more God strengthened me and removed hindrances. I completed the tasks that I started, which seemed to remove feelings of loneliness, and my season changed.

Understanding the cause and triggers of loneliness is essential to overcoming it. My realization that another person will not cure the internal emptiness and voids comforts me during my seasons of loneliness. I've learned to enjoy my own company and appreciate being with myself. I take myself out to the movies, to dinner, to plays/events, and I take my family of one on vacation every year. I've learned to enjoy the life that God has given me! Singleness is a time of life freedom, and I am learning to seize these moments.

I've also found that serving others brings a lasting sense of fulfillment that can never be replaced. Discovering my God-given purpose and launching into that purpose is truly a satisfying life. Many people are lonely and dissatisfied because they are not living on purpose, and they are in constant pursuit of a lot of things that God did not call them to. These things are not always bad things and are most times good things, but they are just not the things that God has called them to. Living life on purpose results in contentment and fulfillment, which negates loneliness. I have learned that it is not possible to be fulfilled and lonely at the same time.

Season of Dating

The dating season is one of the most complex and emotional fluctuating seasons that a single endures. Because of the broad perceptions of dating, its definition has become fluid and boundless. When someone asks me on a date, I don't know if that means dinner and a movie or if it's an invitation for a sexual encounter. I don't know if the invitation means they're interested in getting to know me or if their girlfriend is busy that night, and I'm a surrogate in her absence. I get exhausted trying to figure out the intent of a person who shows interest, and it discourages me from wanting to date at all. As a person who desires marriage, not dating is probably not the best option. The question becomes, how do I date successfully? How do I get to know someone before my emotions are tied to the person? Welcome to the dating season! I am by no means a dating expert nor do I proclaim to know all the answers. I am in the midst of a journey of understanding the answers to these questions, but I will share what I have learned through my experiences and failures. Albert Einstein stated that failure is success in progress, so I've learned to appreciate the failed relationships and seize them as learning experiences that are grooming me for a successful relationship.

Oftentimes, Christian dating results in a battle between flesh and spirit. Our flesh desires intimacy, both emotionally and physically, and our spirits desires spirituality and strength. Paul said that the good he wants to do just doesn't happen, and the bad that he plans not to do seems to always happen (Romans 7:19). Isn't that a familiar feeling when it comes to dating in today's society? Paul's struggle in this text was between his flesh and his spirit. Whether it's an emotional battle of not being able to handle being alone or a physical battle of fleshly desire to obtain momentary sexual fulfillment, the fleshly pull is there. Most singles, including Christians, regularly engage in premarital sex. Not engaging in sexual activities seems strange to most people. I have been on a first date with a guy who is surprised that I won't have sex with him. It blows my mind that the sanctity of something so sacred is being treated so recklessly. Sex is like fire. When fire is in a controlled environment, such as a fireplace, it provides comfort, warmth, and enjoyment. However, when fire is not controlled, it becomes dangerous and destructive to everything in its path. Marriage serves as a fireplace that controls the danger and destruction of sex, and when it leaves that boundary of marriage, destruction will soon follow.

I realize that practicing abstinence until marriage is much easier said than done, especially in the sex-craved society that we live in today. Nonetheless, Christian singles must trust God's word and believe that He will sustain (Psalm 54:4) during times of temptation. He will not allow more than we can bear, and He will always make a way of escape (1 Corinthians 10:13). I have learned that the real temptation is to resist the temptation of being tempted. For example, a female going over a boyfriend's house late at night to watch TV is the temptation. Not going is resisting the temptation to be tempted. The Bible says to resist the devil and he will flee (James 4:7), but when dealing with lust, the scripture says to *run* (2 Timothy 2:22). I am not a virgin and am by no means an expert in abstinence, but I will say that resisting temptations to be tempted has kept me for many years. Yes, *years*! The good news is that God has kept me, but the disappointing news is that men have left me! Sometimes it feels as though God's plan for relationships does not work in today's society, and I've missed opportunities of having a relationship by following God's plan. God then reminded me that having sex with someone does *not* guarantee commitment or a good relationship but habitually leads to heartache, disappointments, and a vicious cycle of sexual misconduct that weakens relationship with Him.

The godly person that God wants to bring will not base the relationship on sexual satisfaction, but it will be based on internal substance, such as integrity, character, and shared core values. This is the substance that will sustain the relationship over time. Taking the stance of abstinence requires the willingness and peace to walk alone. It requires the tenacity to try again if failure occurs and temptation conquers during moments of weakness. The key is to not make permanent decisions like marriage just to subdue the desires of the flesh. Lust is not limited to sex, which means that marriage will not cure the lust. Marriage will only redirect the lust into other areas, which is why it's important to deal with the lust and not only its symptoms. I've also learned not to be too quick to broadcast a lifestyle of abstinence. Every time I've made that declaration up front, I became a personal quest. It's not worth the battles of being quested and not loved. When I was quested, I started getting all the "I love you" and the warm and fuzzies to make me believe that the relationship was in a place that it really wasn't. The goal wasn't to build a relationship but to get me so emotionally tied into the lies until I would be willing to do anything for them. I have now decided to leave out the detail of abstinence until I get to know the person and it seems that we may have a chance of moving forward in a relationship. I've learned that by merely not having sex on the first date eliminates a lot of people. They move on to someone else, which is always for my good! There is no good thing that God will withhold from those who walk upright (Psalm 84:11). I do believe that there is a happy balance between dating and not dating, and I admit that I'm still trying to find that balance.

As I mentioned earlier, I desire marriage, but I hate dating. I've included a few of my experiences that have assisted in establishing my lack of desire for dating.

The urine sample

This guy lived a few doors down from me and was a welcoming face when I first moved in. Because we lived in such close proximity, we would talk almost daily. His patio was in eyesight of my patio, and I would sit with him on his patio from time to time. Soon enough, the conversation led to an invitation for sex, not even one date. Because I turn down the sexual invitation, he immediately dismissed me and asked me to leave. A few days later, he pulls the cables out my cable box. I called the cable company to have the cable restored, but a few days later, he pulled them out again. The cable technician had to put a lock on the box to prevent future occurrences. Days later, he knocks on my door and asks me to give him $5.00 for gas, which I did not give him. A few days later, he knocks on my door holding an empty urine sample cup in his hand. He asked me to fill it with my urine so that he could pass a drug test for work. I closed the door in his face and pretended that I never knew him.

The mind-blower

This guy was very sweet, loved God, and always respected me. I thought this was the one, and he often talked about getting married and starting a family. He lived out of state and usually came to my city to visit me. After months of dating, I decided to make my first visit to his house. I felt that I could never really know him until I was able to experience his environment and how he lived on a daily basis. It was then that I learned that he believed that his boss was hiding behind garbage cans and mailboxes on his street watching him. I looked out the window, and no one was there. Oh, but that's because "he was hiding." He did not have a landline phone in the house only because he believed people were listening in on his calls. However, no one ever listened in on his cell phone? He believed people were looking through his windows and always watching him. It was truly a mind-blowing experience. In addition to these experiences, I learned that he was still in relationship with an ex-girlfriend that he promised he stopped communicating with, and he was still paying the cell phone bill for a different ex-girlfriend because she needed help. Needless to say, this relationship was over, and that was my first and last visit.

The atheist

I reconnected with an old friend, and we hung out and had a great time together. He actually appreciated the fact that I did not have sex with him after the first date. He said that he could trust me and seemed extremely happy with my standards. As we continued to see each other, he began questioning statements that I make, such as, "I thank God for _____." He asked me why was I always thanking God for everything that I accomplished. I told him that I was only able to accomplish what I have by the strength and grace of God. Revelation of his lack of belief in God begins to uncover—atheist. Oddly enough, he didn't want to call himself an atheist, but he put God in the category of Santa Claus. Because I became emotionally tied to him, I attempted to compromise in order to keep the relationship. Eventually, the needed compromises continued to increase on my end. He began to refuse to visit me on the weekends if I went to church. I didn't try to make him go to church, but that wasn't enough. He gave me a choice to stay home and see him or go to church and not see him. I chose to continue going to church, and the relationship dissipated.

The professional

I dated this guy in hopes that it would lead to a lasting relationship. He always gave me the needed attention and focus. Whenever I needed to talk to him, he made the time. He would stop whatever he was doing to make sure I was okay. After a few months of dating, people who knew him would ask me questions about his relationship with his son's mother. I didn't think much about it at first, but after frequent inquests, I began to wonder what was really going on. So I asked him if he paid child support, and he told me that he didn't because he takes care of his son and provides him with everything that he need. I started digging into the reasoning behind not paying child support, which really ticked him off. I found a button to push, and I pushed it as far as I could. Finally, he confessed that he lived with his son and, of course, his son's mother. After my continued questioning, he reveals that he was still in relationship with his son's mother. He told me that he is a professional black man, a rare commodity, and he had a pool of women who were accessible to him. He wasn't going to choose only one woman, and no one with his available options would. He in turn gave me an ultimatum, deal with it or move on. He also warned me that *every* man cheats, so moving on would not do me any good. Nevertheless, I moved on.

These are only a few examples of dating experiences that I've had. Disappointment after disappointment left my heart bitter and cold, and I stopped giving anyone a chance to disappoint me again. I embraced singleness as the final chapter of my life and began to believe that it would never change. I questioned myself time and time again and wondered why I am attracting the wrong people. As you can see from my examples, it's never the same type of man. I've heard that if you always attract the same type of person, then it's something about you that's magnetizing that personality type. I have no words for what I've attracted because it's all different. The only rationale I have is that varying temptations prepares for varying blessings. Nonetheless, it's discouraging, and the older I get, the options become more limited. Many singles my age have been married and divorced and are still broken from previous marriages. They do not allow themselves time to heal before jumping into a new relationship. Broken people are like broken pieces of glass. Anyone who touches the broken pieces are at risk of being cut, hurt, and wounded. Consequently, I try to avoid dating men who are recently divorced, thus limiting the dating pool even more.

I was listening to Joel Osteen on Sirius XM radio when message number 541 was broadcasted. During this message, Joel Osteen, pastor of Lakewood Church, spoke about the blessings of closed doors. Joel Osteen explained how there's a natural proclivity to celebrate the doors that God has opened and to become down and discouraged when doors are closed. He goes on to explain that our closed doors are just as important as every open door. Thus, they should be celebrated as well. God has allowed relationships to fail and the doors to close so that He could redirect me to something better. I always pray, "Lord, if it's not your will, block it," and then I'd get mad when He actually blocks it! I have finally learned to thank God for those closed doors and blocked relationships because I know He has something better for me. Who God has for me is more than what I can handle right now, so He's preparing and maturing me so that I won't mishandle the blessing that He sends to my life. God's thoughts are higher than my thoughts, and His ways are higher than my ways (Isaiah 55:9), and He will do exceedingly and abundantly above all I could ever ask, think, or imagine (Ephesians 3:20).

Expectations

I've heard it said, "You attract who you are," which means it's unrealistic to expect to attract someone who is meeting standards that I am not obtaining or at least in strong pursuit of achieving. Instead, I've decided to take time and effort into becoming the person that I want to attract. For example, I love men who dress well and are clean shaved and carry themselves well. However, I would wake up in the morning feeling tired and sleepy and grab the first clean and comfortable clothing items I could find. I would wonder why none of these men would notice me, and I thought about the law of attraction, that is to attract who you are. Now I put intentional effort into my appearance. The goal is not to be vain, but to become who I want to attract. In doing this, I believe God will send that same kind of person into my life. Just as I want God to send a prepared person to me, I have to become a prepared person for someone else. I've heard people encourage singles to write down what you want in a spouse in reference to Habakkuk 2:2 "write the vision." I understand the intent, but I've been single for 20 plus years, and desires change based on growth, maturity, and age. When I was 20, I didn't mind dating someone who live with their mother and not have a car. After reaching my 40s, I am not interested in anyone who still lives with their mother unless he is helping and assisting. Vision is tied to purpose and calling, and a spouse is someone who should complement the purpose, calling, and vision that God has placed upon your life. Yes, write the vision and make it plain (Habakkuk 2:2), but I'm learning to link those characteristics to the vision and the purpose that God has set for my life. Once purpose has been sought and discovered, I believe that God will send the destined person to come along side to enhance and compliment that purpose. I know people who have "written" down the description of the future spouse, and met someone who met all the check marks that they wrote, but their list did not consider all the apparent deficiencies that the individual had in areas outside of their checkboxes, which led the relationship into a sorrowful and quick divorce. I believe God will direct the right person at His appointed time. Scripture says to "seek *first* the kingdom of God and *all* these things will be added unto you (Matthew 6:33). Christians often talk about divine connections when it comes to jobs, business deals, and new ventures, but we neglect to link "divine connections" to God connecting us to the right person who will become our lifelong partner. I believe that God will divinely connect the right people at the right time.

I've met people who became a close friend during specific seasons in my life, but over time, we don't talk as much, and the relationship drifts away. No one is mad or upset. It's just the season changed. The same scenario often happens in dating relationships, but it's easy to become so anxious and fearful of being alone until the natural progression of separation is lost, and there is pressure to keep pushing together what's drifting away. Some people come into my life for a season, some for a reason, and only a few will enter for a lifetime. I know women who will meet a man today, and in their mind, they've planned the wedding, bought the house, named the children, and planned retirement well before the first date! So when the date actually happens and it goes sour, this woman is now devastated; her wedding, her house, and her future children have all dissipated! As hilarious as this sounds, it's a reality for many women, and this mourning leads her into a phase of grieving over something that was never even there! When I was in my twenties, I was this woman, which is why I can relate to the devastation of an imaginary loss.

I have learned how to enjoy the journey of singleness and appreciate the encounters, both good and bad, and understand that everything happens for a reason (Romans 8:28). Just as I have friends who come in and out of my life, I may date people who will come and then go. I don't expect someone to magically be this perfect person, and instantly, we'll live happily ever after. When I meet someone new, I have learned to take time to pray and seek God for understanding of their purpose in my life. Some people I dated have shown me joys of having a partner, and others have shown me weaknesses and issues within myself that I need to resolve. Joel Osteen often says, "Don't waste your pain." Failed relationships can become blessings by aiding in the preparation to receive the gift that God is preparing. Experiencing a lot of rainy days makes me appreciate the sunshine, and sometimes the bad and failed relationships are only cultivating appreciation for the good relationship when it arrives. One day, my dating relationship will evolve to a union of two purposes by which God will confirm. I will then have the desire of my heart, the fulfillment of my vision, my lifelong partner, my spouse!

Season of Revelation

One night while attending a church service, a prophetic anointing began to manifest in the pastor, and he began speaking prophetically to several individuals regarding specific situations. He moved through the room, and soon enough, the pastor made his way to me. He told me that I was doing the same thing over and over again, like a revolving door, and God wants to break the cycle. He then moved to the next person. At the time, I recently started a new job with a different company, and things appeared to be changing a lot in my life. Consequently, I listened and respected the declaration, but I didn't really think too much of it because I felt that it didn't apply to me at that time in my life. However, a few days passed, and I clearly saw the revolving door!

Satan will portray himself in a way that provokes believers to believe a lie. There are times when the truth becomes blurred and skewed by deep internal hopes and desires of the lie becoming a reality. Sounds strange to actually desire and hope in a lie, but it's true for many. For instance, some people remain in an abusive relationship because of their hope and desire in the lie of "I love you" from their abuser. People hold on to toxic relationships in hopes that the desire to be loved, valued, and accepted by that individual will one day become a reality. Satan is very attentive to those desires and creates imitations of manifestation in a way that is deceptive and mimics truth. Satan will provide an inner feeling that counterfeits the prompting of the Holy Spirit to provide an illusion of God's direction. It is the still small voice that is commonly associated with the leading of God, which leads and directs us to the intended path. However, 1 John 4:1 says not to believe every spirit but test the spirit and see if it is of God. The spirits are not tested by acting on what the voice or prompting is telling us to do but by validating what the spirit says in accordance to the word of God. God will never contradict his word and will never speak to his people in a way that's contrary to it. The next predecessor of God's leading is a comforting peace, not hurt, depression, fear, belittlement, or discouragement. Now let's see how this relates to my revolving door.

I had a male friend whom I found to be very attractive and fun to be around. Although I was his friend, I desired to be more. Eventually, I got enough courage to express to him how I felt. He never confirmed his feelings one way or another, which indirectly confirmed that he did not feel the same way. So I respected the friendship enough to continue as his friend and accepted the realization that there would never be anything more. As friends, we had many heartfelt conversations. We shared dreams, visions, aspirations, as well as hurts, pains, and desires to change the world! I shared many intimate moments with him, never physical, as I never lost awareness that he dated many women and had other female friends.

Because I didn't have physical intimacy with him, I believed that I would not develop soul ties and that the friendship would remain innocent and harmless. However, I quickly learned that soul ties are not contingent upon physical intimacy, but they will develop by sharing the most intimate part of yourself to someone else. I define a soul tie as a transfer of spirits from one person to another. Because I had been very intimate with him by sharing my innermost feelings, thoughts, and emotions, I developed a soul tie, a spiritual transfer of myself to him. I found myself always accessible as a consistent supporter assisting with anything that he needed. I tried to do whatever I could to make his life easier and more productive in attempt to push his aspirations and dreams into reality. However, he never reciprocated this support for me. He would make promises to assist me with projects but never followed through. When I initiated a call to talk to him, sometimes he would answer the call, and other times he wouldn't, but I would always answer when he called me. In spite of his lack of reciprocation, I believed in the false desires and hope that one day he would appreciate my generosity and reciprocate the same loyalty and support that I've so graciously given to him. There was a small voice on the inside telling me to pursue and to be that one consistent and steady person in his life, which I initially believed to have been God.

After the special service and the prophetic word was spoken to me, I was having a conversation with him and saw the repeated behaviors that had now cycled for years. I then realized that he was my revolving door! I have been circling this door for over three years and arrived nowhere. It was clear that he had no intentions of pursuing a relationship with me, and he was not a friend to me. I then began to question (test) the validity of the inner voice that I heard before telling me to pursue, and God began to reveal His word to me in scripture, which He never contradicts. He showed me 1 Corinthians 13:4–8, which states that love is not self-seeking and always protects. I asked God to show me more. God then showed me John 15:13, which states God has no greater love than to lay down his life for a friend. None of these characteristics aligned with this guy that I tried to convince myself was my friend. Based on the scriptural definition of a friend, he was not my friend, and the prophecy spoken over my life was fully confirmed. My mind was totally blown away as to how something that seem so minimal could be so significant. I thought this innocent friendship was a divine connection that God was using to prepare a relationship, but in truth, it was Satan using manipulation to create a false and blurred perception of a yearned reality. Satan took the inner hopes and desires to bridge a stronghold that kept me in a cycle of emotional highs and lows. I'm thankful that I serve Jehovah Mephalti (Psalms 18:2), the God who delivers!

As a single, it's common to have high hopes that the next date will be the lifelong partner that's deeply desired. If we're not careful, we'll get stuck in the journey and never reach the destination. My first road trip from Mississippi to Chicago was super exciting. I was a child and had never been far from home. I didn't conceptualize the true distance of the journey until the journey was in progress. Every time we embarked a pass-through town, I'd get excited and ask, "Are we there yet?" If I was in control of the drive, I most likely would have ended the trip in one of the pass-through towns along the way and missed the destination. Thankfully, those driving were aware that we were several hours and hundreds of miles into our trip but knew that the passing towns were not the destination. Thus, they continued the journey regardless of my restlessness and anxiousness. As singles on a journey toward marriage, it's easy to get distracted with the pass-throughs, but regardless of the restlessness and anxiousness, it's imperative to stay the course and not miss the destination because of distractions (pass-throughs) along the way. God has started us on the journey toward the destination of marriage (for those desiring to be married), and we cannot stop at the first nice town (man/woman) along the way because we're tired of the journey.

Dr. Tony Evans defines success as the arrival at a prescribed destination. God has a prescribed destination for every area of our lives, including relationships. If we stay on God's path, test the spirits by the word of God, and not settle for the pass-throughs, then we'll achieve success and reach our God prescribed destination.

Season of Preparation

*T*he season of preparation is a time to discover and pursue purpose. It's a time when internal conflicts and identity struggles will surface, but it's merely the launching pad for discovering truth and identity through Christ.

Self-identity

As a single, I often feel isolated, unsupported, and weighed down by life. The pursuit to accomplish goals somehow becomes a lone-ranger voyage that feels as though I'm at war and it's me against the world. The tolerance of negative thoughts, beliefs, and experiences are underlying culprits driving negative perceptions and ultimately negative actions. Perception is often limited to exposure and understanding. That is, my perception is my truth until I'm exposed to something different and another truth is revealed. I remember receiving my first pair of eyeglasses when I was about twelve years of age, and I felt as though I had entered a new world or dimension; it was a twilight-zone experience! The fact is, my environment had not changed, but the perception through which I was now able to see the world around me was drastically different. This is the same experience I had when I stopped viewing the world through my personal experiences and beliefs and began to see the world through God's eyes, everything changed! For example, I felt very unloved and unwanted as a child, and it birthed an underlying conviction that I'm never truly accepted and loved by others. Consequently, my belief was that people only talked to me because they either wanted something from me or they had no one else to talk to. However, I got new lenses through the word of God.

Romans 12:4–5 allowed me to see that believers are all one body, and each member belongs to the other. I began to see that I have a place, and I belong to the body of Christ. I started believing and accepting what God says about me: He says that I'm fearfully and wonderfully made (Psalm 139:14), He formed me (Psalm 139:13), and He made mention of me before I was born (Isaiah 49:1). God intends for me to be prosperous and to have good success (Joshua 1:8). His plans are not to harm me but give me an expected end (Jeremiah 29:11). God is intentional in all that He does, and even when it seems I'm alone and unsupported, the Lord is with me (1 Chronicles 22:18) and has ordered my steps (Psalm 37:23).

Self-perception directly links to self-identity. Mistaken identity is the number one thief that robs individuals of manifesting their gifts and talents given by God. So many dreams, talents, and gifts are lying in weight in graves because individuals never accepted who they were, which stagnated the birth of their talents. Many people become imitators of someone else and never seek to find out who they really are.

I heard a story of a young man who admired an older guy who seemed to be cool, calm, and collective at all times. This guy wore the latest fashion, had the cutest girls, hung out with the coolest guys, and always seemed to have the most adventurous experiences. The young man desired so much to be like this guy until he spent a lot of time studying this guy's life, everything from his schedule and habits to demeanor and jargon, so that he could become just like him. This older guy never noticed his younger admirer who longed to have just one face-to-face conversation with him. Finally, the young guy had his long-awaited opportunity to speak with the older guy, and he asked him questions about his life and how he became so accomplished. The older guy began to tell the younger guy how he admired someone else who had everything that he wanted, and he started mimicking everything about the other person in hopes of becoming just like him. After all the studying, following, and determination to be like someone else, the young guy learned that he was pursuing a copycat reflection of another individual. No doubt that individual followed the footsteps of someone before him, and the cycle goes on and on from person to person until someone decides to finally be an original.

Jesus gave an example through a parable, real-life examples of biblical truths, written in Matthew 25:14–30. The parable states that a master has to take a long trip, and he leaves his talents with his workers. He distributes the talents among the workers based on their abilities. One worker receives five talents, another two talents, and the other worker received one talent. The workers receiving the five and two talents invested and doubled what the owner gave them. However, the worker who received only one talent buried it. When the owner returned, the first two workers showed the owner how they maximized the talents that were given to them, and they were praised for their faithfulness. Because they were faithful over the little, the owner declared that he would make them ruler over much. The worker given only one talent tells the owner that he buried the one talent out of fear and returned the one talent that was given. The owner told him that he could have at least deposited the talent in the bank to gain interest. The owner deemed him as being wicked and took the one talent from him and gave it to the other workers. The owner in this parable is said to be God, and the workers are the believers who follow Him.

God gives His believers talents (abilities) that he expects to be maximized during our time on earth. When we show faithfulness over the small things that He give us, He will begin to increase us with more. However, if we bury the talents/gifts that He has given us, then we rob Him of manifestation within the earth. Being who God has called me to be is greater than my personal feelings, but it's about maximizing God's purpose on the earth. Every time my talent is used and someone grows closer to God, then the talent has returned an increase into the kingdom!

God has created us on purpose and for purpose. Jeremiah 29:11 states, "For I know the plans I have for you, says the Lord, plans to prosper you and not to harm you." There are billions of people on planet earth, yet no two people have the same fingerprints. Each of us are unique, and our fingerprints are God's stamp of distinction on each of us. Trying to follow and mimic another person will only lead to a life of constant searching and never fulfillment. When I decided to be an original, the pressure of trying to be accepted, admired, and approved by others ceased. I learned that the only approval I need has already been provided by my heavenly Father, and his love is never failing (Psalm 89:33) (1 Corinthians 13:8). It's amazing to know that the same God who controls the universe accepts and loves me just the way I am. He loved me enough to die so that I might be saved! With that type of support, it doesn't really matter what others think or have to say about me. I am a child of the King, the most-high God, and there is no devil in hell that can stop or change that!

I have learned to continually seek affirmation and guidance from God and not from people. People did not create me; God did, which means they don't know my intended purpose. If someone purchases a new Infiniti car and it suddenly begins to malfunction, the owner is not going to take the car to a Chevy service shop for repair. However, they are going to take the car back to the manufacturers, specialists, and creators of that particular car. The car owner knows that Chevy technicians may not know why certain wires were placed in certain places and may not quite understand the intentions of key features and functions of that vehicle. Christians, by which all things are made new (2 Corinthians 5:17), have the tendency to take what God created, which is ourselves, to be serviced by others who were not involved in our creation and will not fully understand the capability, features, or intent of our lives. Consequently, going to people to service my purpose will limit capabilities and can lead to abuse.

Misuse or reallocation of a person or thing from its intended purpose is abuse. For example, turning a piano into a dining-room table is technically abuse to the piano because it's functioning outside of its intended purpose, which is to be played and to release sounds of music. The end result of abuse is teardown and destruction of the abused person or thing. As the piano sits as a dinner table not being tuned, played, and utilized for its purpose, its functionality will eventually weaken. The keys will start sticking together, and even if someone tries to play it, the sound wouldn't be right because it hasn't been tuned and readjusted for its proper use. The same is true for Christians. When we're not fulfilling the purpose that God has created us to fill, we're just like that piano being used as a dinner table. We've limited ourselves to exterior eloquence without any regard to the full purpose and potential that's on the inside. We're going to church but without purpose; we're wearing the latest fashion but no purpose and are empty and void on the inside. Living outside our God-given purpose can be considered abuse, the misuse or reallocation from intended purpose, to gifts (talents) that God has given.

As I began pursuit of purpose and ways to maximize my talents, it became imperative to rely on God as a sustainer. There are times when finances can become limited, and it's tempting to falter and reinterpret the word of God. I remember separating from my first full-time job and had no income. I didn't know how I was going to pay rent, car payment, utilities, groceries, etc. It wasn't long before I was offered a proposition by a man who only wanted to spend time with me, so he said. He was a retired school teacher who offered to pay my car payments, to give me spending money, and to take care of any financial needs that I had. The only requirement was to go out to dinner with him. He was in his late sixties to early seventies, and I was in my early twenties. He said that he only wanted my company and nothing else. As tempting as this proposition was during this vulnerable time for me, I turned down the offer so that this man would not be my source, and I'd continue to trust God as my source and sustainer! This guy insisted that I took his phone number just in case I changed my mind. To avoid any temptations, I immediately discarded the number and looked to Jehovah Jireh, the God who provides (Genesis 22:14).

Prostitution is not limited to the woman on the street corner, but it's any act of receiving cash for sexual favors. Sadly, many prostitutes sit in church Sunday after Sunday hearing the word of God, but instead of trusting the God that they talk about, they choose to fulfill favors to men to get their bills paid. I admit that I had some rough times, but I never went without food, clothes, shelter, transportation, and gas in my car, and *all* my needs were met! It was God who sustained me and provided my needs during that time. God showed me that He can be trusted, and all I have to do is depend on Him. Even today, I realize that everything I have accomplished has been by His grace. Matthew 26:6 reads, "Look at the birds. They do not plant or harvest or store food in barns, for your heavenly father feeds them. And aren't you far more valuable to him than they are?" God will never allow his children to stumble and fall (2 Peter 1:10). He only needs His people to trust in Him and recognize that He is the source.

Money management

Preparation is also a season of generating revenue and managing the resources. I strive to always know where my money is going because it helps me to better control where it goes. I have been in situations where I received extra money, such as a bonus at work or a tax refund, and had no idea where the money went. This happened because my spending wasn't planned, and if it's not planned, then it's vulnerable to being wasted on fruitless purchases and momentary gains. Ben Franklin is credited with quoting the statement, "If you fail to plan, you are planning to fail." This same truth is evident and proven when managing and spending money. I've heard people say that they don't have a lot of money, so there's nothing to budget, but because you don't have a lot of money, it's more critical to have a budget to ensure control of where the cash flows.

Pete the Planner, renown columnist for *USA Today* and is considered to be one of the best personal financial experts in the nation, challenged himself to limit his weekly transactions to only ten transactions per week, which includes cash, debit, and credit card transactions. This practice reveals just how frequently cash flows out of our possession on a weekly basis and forces self-reflection of how much money is truly being spent in a week's time. This challenge may sound simple, but it's much easier said than done. It was very surprising for me to learn just how frequently I was making financial transactions. Reducing the frequency of spending can but does not guarantee a reduction in overall spending and ultimately increase available cash. It's kind of like leaving a water faucet in the house on and running water all day; it may not flood your house, but it will definitely increase the water bill.

Another method of cash flow control that I use is the cash method. I give myself a spending budget for the week and take only that amount out of my account in cash. Everything that I buy during the week has to be purchased using my allocated cash. Because I'm a very visual person, it triggers something for me to see my dollars slowly drift away, which decreases my spending. For some reason, using a debit card and not physically seeing the cash reduction somehow tricks my mind into thinking that I can spend more! Consequently, the cash-only spending method brings awareness of money leaving my possession, and it helps me to better evaluate the significance and need for each purchase.

There are many different methods to reduce spending, and I am by no means a financial expert, but I know that spending less and saving more prepares me for unexpected financial expenses, such as car repairs, home repairs, unforeseen health conditions, job loss, etc. Unexpected financial events *will happen*, so it's imperative to plan and prepare for them. The more prepared I am to handle unexpected financial expenses, the less vulnerable I become to needing favors for help.

Singles who desire to be married should also prepare a favorable financial situation for a future spouse. My goal is to create the type of financial situation that I want to come into. It's often stated and proven that we attract who we are. Because I don't want my future spouse to be broke, I use this time of preparation to ensure that I'm not broke. I am always open to seeking professional counseling on how to better manage finances, and they've given me great strategies on how to balance investments and spending. My former pastor always teaches the principle of delayed gratification, which simply means that we don't have to have it all right now. Sometimes we have to save over time so that we can comfortably make big purchases or take elaborate vacations. Learning to preserve in the now has allowed me to reap later. I will have to live in my future; therefore, I'm preparing the financial future that I want to live in.

In addition to monitoring spending habits, I've learned the significance and importance of protecting my income and assets. If an unexpected injury, surgery, or an unplanned event occurs that significantly impacts my income, I need to have my assets covered. I'm fortunate to work for an employer who provides critical illness, accidental injury, and hospitalization insurance, which can cover my mortgage, car payments, and basic necessities if either of these events occur. Short-term and long-term disability insurance only pays a percentage of regular accrued income, which is why I chose to opt in additional coverage. If my employer did not offer these benefits, I would acquire this insurance from a third-party insurance carrier. If the unexpected happens, I want to have supplemental funds to cover basic monthly expenses without emptying my savings until I'm able to resume a normal work schedule. One sickness or injury can be detrimental to financial stability. Consequently, I pay for the extra insurance coverage to protect the things that have taken me years to obtain.

Life insurance is another way to protect income and assets. It's far too common for someone to pass away, and living relatives have to come together and figure out how to pay for funeral arrangements. Because my mother is retired and do not keep continuous coverage, I purchased a small term policy for her, just in case. Of course, I would like for her to live forever, but death is inevitable. Because it's inevitable, some things should be in place to manage it when it arrives. As a single, I ensure that I have a basic policy that will cover funeral cost as well as an accidental death policy so that my family won't have a financial burden of burying me. Because I do not have children and I am the only person dependent on my income, I've chosen basic coverage. However, if I had children or a spouse who depends on my income, I would choose a policy that would allocate enough funds to assist in covering those expenses as well.

Last but definitely not least, tithing and sowing are critical components to managing financial resources. As a Christian, tithing is not an option! I have heard many Christians debate the philosophy of tithing and argue that tithing was a principle of the law per the Old Testament, but I know the proven truth in my life. I have sacrificed paying bills in order to pay tithes, and God has never failed me. In the book of Malachi 3:10, God says, "Try me, or test me, in this and see don't I pour you out a blessing." Well, I have tried, and I have seen the blessings of God manifest in my life. I remember choosing to pay tithes and not having enough left to pay my car payment, and within a few days, I received a check in the amount of the car payment from the bank that financed the car. It stated that I could use this check as my monthly payment whenever I wanted to use it. I remember times when I was without a job and had to pay rent, utilities, etc., and God always provided and somehow gave me everything that I needed. After I established an unshakable trust in God to provide my needs, He began providing me with increase beyond my needs. I continue to tithe and sow monetary seeds into the lives of others whenever possible, and God continues to increase me financially.

My former pastor often challenges his congregation with the question, "Is God worth a dime?" At the end of the day, we're talking about a dime on a dollar, and our actions reflect whether or not we believe He's truly worth a dime. Sowing financial seeds is not limited to giving offerings in church, but I've been in line behind someone in the grocery store who comes up a little short of having enough to pay their bill, and it's no better feeling than to pay the remaining balance for them. I've sown into college students who live on campus with no job and no money to buy the things that they need. Giving food and clothes to families in need are also ways of sowing. The scripture says that those who give to the poor lends to God (Proverbs 19:17), and we know that God will not let anyone be in debt to him. The more I give, the more I receive.

A familiar scripture that is often quoted with a negative connotation is "You reap what you sow" (Galatians 6:7), but when I'm sowing good things, this scripture is comforting by reminding me that I will get back all the things that I'm sowing. I've also learned that sowing should not be limited to people who are less fortunate than me, but I should sow into people who have arrived where I'm trying to go. While trying to write a book, I've purchased books written by people I know even if it's not relatable to me as a way of sowing into their success. Because I've sown into their books, I expect to reap a published book. When I sow into people operating in places and spaces where I want to go, I'm setting myself up for that situation to manifest in my life as I will reap what I sow!

Serving

Preparation is also a time of service, which is the act of providing someone with something needed or desired. As a single, especially having no children, it's easy to become self-serving without regard to the needs and desires of others. Singles with no dependents only have the responsibility of taking care of self, which is an ingredient for a narrow vision that is only focused on self and a selfish way of life. It's possible to live a selfish lifestyle and not be fully aware of the neglect and insensitivity portrayed toward others. Because the only person I'm responsible for is me, it takes a conscious effort to remain aware and supportive of the needs and concerns of others. Because I desire to be married, I believe that understanding the act of serving others is critical in preparing for a spouse.

I believe that serving is a critical component to having a healthy and happy relationship. To maintain awareness in an attempt to minimize or even eliminate self-service, I look for ministries and organizations that will allow me to volunteer and serve others! I do know people who will join a ministry or organization for personal gains, such as recognition, benefits, or to gain notary acts for job placement or college enrollment. However, that taints the service principle. Consequently, I look for opportunities that are of no benefit to me but enhances the lives of others—that's service. Ministry and community outreach organizations are great venues for learning how to serve others. These organizations ignite sacrifices of our two most valuable resources, time and/or money. Not only does these sacrifices serve a greater good to recipients, but they also dismantle selfishness by putting care and concern to action for something and somebody other than myself. Volunteering generates a deeper appreciation for daily blessings that I often overlooked, and it links me to something greater than myself.

Balance

Preparation is also a season of establishing balance among conflicting demands in life. Serving has been great for me because it keeps my mind focused on something other than my personal issues and concerns, and it assists in revealing purpose in my life. However, religious organizations oftentimes target singles to take on greater responsibilities because we are perceived to have more available time due to the lack of family responsibilities. Although I do not have obligations to a spouse or children, I've learned that I still have to balance my life. As a single, I still have the responsibility to pay bills, do laundry, clean the house, buy grocery, go to work, take care of home repairs, take care of car repairs, and everything else that comes with being an adult. I've had ministry leaders tell me to travel and see the world and to go out and enjoy life but become anxious of who's going to complete my tasks when I actually leave for vacation. Or they think I'm upset or offended when I exercise my right to say no to a request of service that will off-balance my life.

I served diligently for many years, and it took me to a place where I had no balance. I began to dread going to church because I had so many responsibilities that distracted me from my purpose of being there. There was consistently one demand after another and one expectation after another. I became so bogged down with *serving* until my spiritual wellness was suffering. I attended church multiple times a week, but I couldn't hear and receive the word being preached because I was distracted by the woes of serving in the ministry. I became a victim of what I call the Martha Syndrome.

Luke 10:38 records the story of Martha who offered her home to Jesus to stay and rest from his travel. When Jesus arrived, Mary, Martha's sister, sat at the feet of Jesus, listening to him teach. However, Martha was preparing food and getting things ready for their guests. Martha sees Mary sitting and becomes angry and asks Jesus to tell Mary to help her. In verse 41, Jesus says, "Martha, Martha, you are worried and upset about many things, but few things are needed—or indeed only one. Mary has chosen what is better, and it will not be taken away from her." Martha was worried about all the things that needed to be done and missed having intimate time with Jesus. This was me; I became victim of *the Martha Syndrome*!

I was working in ministry and had to account for who showed up, who's late, who didn't have what they needed, if the right seats were reserved, if refreshments were in place for guests, if the garbage had been taken out, etc. This was Martha. She was in the presence of Jesus but worried about everything except his presence! Martha was so focused on *things* until she missed the one thing, which was being in the presence of Jesus. It's very easy to get caught up in the due diligence of service and miss the guest of honor, Jesus himself. In the midst of feeling overwhelmed, I learned that there is still room at the feet of Jesus. He was just waiting for me to get there. If a car's alignment is off, the car consistently pulls in one direction. This constant pull wears the tires down quicker, the car burns more gas, and more physical effort is required to hold the car in place while driving. The car can be taken to a mechanic, who can make the necessary adjustments to place everything back into alignment, which results in more gas efficiency and less effort while driving to a destination. The same is true for me! God is my adjuster, and when I allow Him, He will make the necessary adjustments so that I am in alignment and can reach my destination more efficiently and with less effort. When I am in alignment with God, He will direct my paths (Proverbs 3:6) and give me success (Joshua 1:8), and my way will be easy (Matthew 11:30).

It is possible to do good things and be out of balance because those are not the things that God has called me to do. Jesus said only one thing is needed (Luke 10:42), and the apostle Paul writes, "This one thing I do" (Philippians 3:13). I have learned to seek God for direction concerning my *one* thing and push forward in that one thing. In many cases this one adjustment has put my life into balance, and I began to experience the abundant life that's intended for me to experience. John 10:10 states that "I came that they may have and enjoy life, and have it in abundance (to the full, till it overflows)."

Season of Waiting

In today's society, everything is instant and moves at the speed of light. The increased use of electronic and digital devices puts almost everything we want and need at our fingertips. I can go for a walk in the park and tear my shirt, and before I get to my car, I can have a new one ordered. Depending on the time of day the order was made, I can have my torn shirt replaced the same day! This constant and instant access has birthed a mandate for instantaneous results and gratification. However, everything is not instant with God. God's not only concerned about getting a blessing to His people, but He's also concerned about the maintenance of the blessing after its received. Consequently, God prepares us for the blessings that He sends so that we will not lose it and have the ability to maintain it. God has predestined our lives so that everything aligns according to His plans and is manifested at the proper time. Because everything else seems to be instant and right now, I find myself plagued with negative emotions and thoughts trending toward unbelief while waiting for my prayers to be manifested. Consequently, I've learned that I must prepare and adjust for my season of waiting.

When no one interesting has crossed my path and no one has asked me on a date in a while, it seems as though singleness is my final destination. However, I know this is a season of waiting that God has placed me in, and there is a purpose and a plan for me during this season. I am reminded of a song by Travis Green, "He's Intentional," as it centers around Romans 8:28: "All things are working for my good." God is truly intentional, and every victory, every pain, and every perceived missed opportunity is intentional. Romans 8:30 reminds me that God made and designed me, and Ephesians 1:11 proves that He is (and was) aware of what I would want before I knew I would want it. Proverbs 16:9 and Psalm 37:3 reinforce the idea that the Lord orders the steps of a man, which means a man (or woman) who seeks God is never lost or misled, but every path has been planned by God. God tells us in Jeremiah 29:11 that He know the plans that He has for His people, and His plans are good and not evil. Because my life is yielded to God, I know that this season is predestined and ordained by God. As a believer following the precepts of God, I can only be where He wants me to be. Consequently, I don't have to worry about whether I've missed the right person coming into my life or if it's too late for me to meet someone. I have confidence that God has a plan for me that is greater than anything I can plan for myself.

The adversary, Satan, loves to surface during times of waiting to increase doubt and unbelief. However, I've learned to have faith in God is to also have faith in His timing. Whenever I take my mind off the word of God and lose sight of the deity of who God is, I find myself getting caught up in the world around me and a culture that is in total opposition to the standards of God. Satan reminds me of the scarcity of morality and tasks himself with convincing me that a godly single man doesn't exist, or he would be very unattractive and not someone I would desire to spend time with and most definitely not marry. Satan will speak through friends and family members to remind me of my age and the possibility of forever being alone. Satan voices himself through people around me to convince me to settle for the first available man I see because my options are few and limited. Satan sends attacks against my self-esteem and self-worth in attempts to convince me that no one wants to marry me. Satan tries to make me think that if I was prettier, thinner, lighter, etc., then I would not be alone. Thus, the faith fight begins!

As mentioned in the earlier scriptures, God is intentional. For believers, this season is predestined and ordained by God. There is a purpose, and there is a plan. Psalm 27:14 states that we should be happy waiting on the Lord (of good courage), and He will strengthen our hearts. I wondered how to be happy and *wait* as it sounds paradoxical. As a participant in our instantaneous society, there's usually no happiness in waiting. However, God reminded me of the two-hour wait to ride an amazing roller coaster at a theme park. Though there was a two-hour wait, I was excited getting in the line, excited waiting (and taking pictures), and super excited getting on the ride that last only seconds! He also reminded me of my trip from Indiana to California. I was excited getting on the plane, excited during my layover waiting to transfer, and super excited to touch the sands of Pacific Beach, California! God showed me that the expectation and conviction of what's to come is what causes the excitement and joy in the wait. He showed me that the sorrow and weariness of waiting is not about the arrival of the promise, but it's the faith fight to continue to believe what was promised is truly on the other side of the wait.

While waiting for the roller-coaster ride, I never doubted that the ride would be there. While traveling to California, I never doubted that my ocean front room would be available or that the beach would be accessible. Neither the two-hour wait for the amusement park ride nor the extended layover caused my faith to waiver. As I retained my excitement during travels and adventures of what's to come, I have to sustain enough faith in God to know that the promises God gave me, including a spouse, are still available and are accessible to me! If I got tired during my layover to California, gave up, and went back home because I couldn't see the beach, then I'm delaying my destiny, not God! It's so easy to blame God for delays, but I have learned (1) delays are not denials, and (2) God is waiting on me to get in position to receive what He has for me. Every time I speak words that are in opposition to what I'm believing, it's like me taking the next plane home during a layover. What I speak will eventually manifest (Proverbs 18:21). As long as I'm speaking faith and continuing to believe that my promise will manifest, then I will see it. Habakkuk 2:3 states, "Though it (vision) tarry, wait for it for it will surely come and it will not tarry." Talk about an oxymoron! Though it tarry, wait, for it will not tarry! The key principle I've learned out of this statement is that if I'm willing to wait forever, then it's never too long of a wait!

Lastly, waiting is also a time of maturing by which God prepares His people for the things that we're believing for. Most adults would not give a twelve-year-old child keys to their car with the intent to drive. At that age, they are not mature enough for the responsibilities that are associated with driving a vehicle. Once they mature and understand the significance of the responsibility and the dangers of mishandling driving privileges, then they are given the car keys. The same is true with our heavenly Father. Though I want the blessings now, God has to mature me to receive the blessing so that I don't mishandle it, damage it, or cause harm to myself. Consequently, I can trust Romans 4:21 and wait with patience without wavering because I know He who promised is faithful! I can quote Isaiah 40:31 with strong conviction and truth that "They that wait on the Lord shall renew their strength, they shall mount up with wings as eagles; they shall run, and not be weary; and they shall walk, and not faint."

Season of Weariness

*F*or years, my entire adult life, I have been believing God for a husband. The Bible says that it's better to be with someone than to be alone and that one can be overtaken but two can defend themselves (Ecclesiastes 4:9–12). God said that it's not good for man to be alone, so God gave him (Adam) a suitable mate (Eve) (Genesis 2:18). Proverbs states that no good thing will be withhold from those who love Him (Proverbs 84:11), and a man who finds a wife finds a good thing and obtains favor from the Lord (Proverbs 18:22). So I asked God, am I not a good thing? Why am I left alone? Ecclesiastes chapter 4:9–12 describes the security of two versus one, and I ask, why do I not have the assurance and security of two? I am not perfect, but I try my best to walk out the word of God and to make godly choices for my life. However, I'm still alone. I have been negatively talked about for attempting to walk out the principles of God and that abstinence would result in a lasting relationship. I watched the same people who mocked my principles get married and start families while I remain single. This challenges my faith, and I wonder, Can God's way work in the freewill liberal society that we live in today?

The Bible records the testimony of Hannah in the book of 1 Samuel 1:6–7. She was a woman who loved God but could not have a child. Because of Hannah's infertility, a woman named Peninnah continuously mocked and humiliated her for her inability to have a child. Women who could not have children during that time were looked down on by society, and Peninnah made sure that Hannah knew how devalued she was. Year after year, I feel humiliated while watching those who mocked my standards move forward with families, careers, and seemingly everything they want. Don't get me wrong. I'm happy for their successes, but I still can't help but wonder,

What about me, Lord? Hannah went before God praying for a change in her situation, and God opened her womb and gave her a child (1 Samuel 1:9–17). I went before God praying for a change in my situation, but unlike Hannah, nothing seemed to happen. It seems as if God didn't hear my prayers and petitions, or He is ignoring me. I decided that I would find someone on my own without waiting on God because it seemed His way wasn't working. However, nothing I try to do on my own works out, and God reminded me of Sarah. God promised Sarah and Abraham a son, but Sarah was tired of waiting for the promise to come to pass, so she asked her husband, Abraham, to have a child with her servant, Hagar (Genesis 16:1–4). When Hagar became pregnant, Sarah regretted the decision and despised her (Genesis 16:6).

Just as Sarah became weary in waiting, I have often gotten tired and weary in waiting on the promises of God to come to pass. After waiting so long, I started to doubt that it was God speaking, but I was reminded of Sarah again when God reminded her of the promise, and she laughed because so many years had passed, and she was old (Genesis 18:13). I know that God's word is true, and it will not return void (Isaiah 55:11), and He has assured me that I will not always be alone. However, as time continues to pass and the encounters of meeting single men become fewer and further between, I find myself challenged in the space between the promise and the manifestation. God challenged the faith of Sarah and Abraham by asking if they believe that there is anything too hard for Him (Genesis 18:14). God did not allow Sarah's unbelief to stop the promise that He made, and He made the declaration that Sarah would have a son the next year despite her mocking the promise (Genesis 18:14). I love the fact that Abraham asked Sarah why she laughed, and she lied about it and said that she did not laugh (Genesis 18:15). I believe God will bless in such a way that we become embarrassed for doubting what He would do in our lives.

The weary season is not always fostered by the wait of a promise, but it can also be times of crisis. I define crisis as a forced turning point, such as an abrupt change in circumstances or lifestyle that surpasses the efforts of human control. Events such as the loss of a loved one or close friend, a negative health diagnosis, an unexpected job loss, birthing a child with special needs, and any other event that abruptly changes the normal patterns of lifestyle and/or well-being. In Psalms 42, David suffered great loss and fell into a state of depression. He started asking the question, "Why art thou cast down O my soul, and why art thou so disquieted within me?" (Psalm 42:5). David repeated this question several times throughout the psalms until he learned to praise God in spite of it. "For I will yet praise him who is the health of my countenance and my God" (Psalm 43:5).

Isaiah 61:3 gives the charge to put on the garment of praise for the spirit of heaviness! Praise breaks the bondage of weariness and heaviness. Although I cannot change the situation, I can trust God, who is all knowing and intentional in everything that He does and allows to happen. He is Jehovah Rapha, the God who heals (Exodus 15:26); Jehovah Nissi, the God of our banner of victory (Exodus 17:15); Jehovah Jireh, the God who provides (Genesis 22:14); Jehovah Shalom, the God of peace (Judges 6:24); El Elyon, the most-high God (Genesis 14:20)! I began to put my circumstances into the perspective of the God that I serve, and my problems become miniscule. I remind myself that I'm not a physical being but a spiritual being who is having an earthly/physical experience, and this life is not the end for me. I then remind myself that these light and momentary afflictions that I am facing are but for a moment (2 Corinthians 4:17). In comparison to what God is going to bring me into, these afflictions are light. That's good news! The better news is that these afflictions are only momentary! I am designed and equipped to conquer and overcome every affliction and attack that comes at me (Romans 8:37, Luke 10:19). My victory is not limited to the afterlife, but I have been promised victory while I'm still on earth (2 Corinthians 2:14).

Once I changed my perspective on who God made me to be and the power that I have through Christ, the negative thoughts and emotions begin to dissipate, as they did for David in Psalms. I begin to praise God for every good thing that is currently happening in my life, no matter how small. I thank God that I woke up in my right mind. I thank God for a bed to sleep in (even if it's not where

I want to be). I thank God for food (even if it's not what I want to eat). The more I began to thank God for what I do have, the better I began to feel. Praise in its simplest and purest form is "Thank you!" People will often say, "All God wants is a praise." What they're saying is that God wants His people to appreciate what He's already done and simply say "Thank you!" Reflecting on the things that God has done always lifts my spirits, and it reminds me that things could be a lot worse. No matter how bad my situation has been or becomes, it can always be worse. There's someone praying to receive what I currently have.

I frequently volunteered at a local detention center, and it was my turn to lead the lesson for the day. As I entered the gloomy room, the girls were irritated, sleepy, hungry, and really didn't want to be bothered. Attending the session was a way for them to come out of their rooms (cells), so they would usually participate even when they really didn't want to. I brought in construction paper and sticky pictures to represent things they're thankful for so that they could build a *Wall of Thanks*. Of course, the question was asked, "What if I don't have anything to be thankful for?" I asked the young lady to think about the girls who are her age in the hospital fighting cancer. I asked her to think about the girls her age who were kidnapped and traded into sex trafficking. I started giving scenario after scenario of ideas of something to be thankful for. The girls then began to think about where they could be versus where they were, and they began building their *Wall of Thanks*. Now these girls who initially complained about all the negative happenings in their life were then able to see a visual of positive focal points in their lives. I allowed every girl who wanted to share with the group an opportunity to show their *Wall of Thanks* and explain how each image set focus to something that they were thankful for. The once irritated girls were now focused on what was going right in their lives versus what was wrong. Their moods and emotions began to change, and I think I even saw a few smiles.

Whether I've become weary waiting on a spouse or weary dealing with life circumstances, I have learned that God will sustain me. I often reflect on Deuteronomy 30:19, which states, "I have set before you life and death, blessing or cursing: therefore, choose life." I decide to choose life when I decide to make thankfulness and gratitude my focus instead of focusing on the negative things happening around me. A famous quote by Charles R. Swindell is that "life is 10% what happens to you and 90% how you respond." Sounds very similar to Deuteronomy 30:19—choose life!

Season of Satisfaction

Merriam-Webster's online dictionary defines the word *satisfy* as one's source of accepted truth. In turn, my beliefs and accepted truth can result in satisfaction. I have seen an unattractive person believe that they are attractive, and their confidence causes those around them to adopt a similar belief. Their accepted truth soon becomes their reality. This same principle can be applied to every area of life. For example, when my financial resources were low, I believed that all my needs would be met based on Philippians 4:19, and my accepted truth became my reality. Because there is no lack financially, I have satisfaction in that area. I do not believe satisfaction is acquired through a ten-step program nor do I believe that it's a mystical place that is visited every once in a while. I believe that satisfaction is a mindset of becoming and eventually being what I've accepted as truths in my heart.

I have defined my accepted truths based on God's principles and promises but sometimes find it challenging to remain in a state of satisfaction. As I began to dig deeper, I learned that my problem wasn't the accepted truth of what could be, but it was rooted in negative self-perceptions. Because the core of satisfaction is based on a *perception* of truth, it's easier to associate the promises of God to others but difficult to accept that truth for my personal life. I've often heard teachings on the obtainment of blessings in the context of "Ten steps to receiving God's blessings" or "How to get your prayers answered," etc. I've also heard to sow toward what you're believing for, and in turn, initiate prayer lines based on specific dollar amounts, which implies that only those sowing that dollar amount will be blessed. If my blessing is solely based on my next step or my next sow (works), then what if I mess up? Will I not be blessed?

What I've learned is that Satan will manipulate perception to bring confusion and unbelief through the varying methods and hypothesis of *how to get your blessings*. I am keenly aware of my personal challenges, failures, and inability to always make the right decisions, and hearing a ten-step process often highlights those inadequacies. When I feel that I've failed at step one, I start to accept a truth that I'm disqualified to receive blessings from God. As a result, I find myself believing for others and doubting for myself. I remember hearing Bishop T. D Jakes, senior pastor of the Potter's House church located in Dallas, Texas, talk about the countless manifestations of miracles that occur during their outreach services in Kenya. Someone asked, "Why is it that new believers in Christ often see more manifestations of God's blessing than those who's been in the faith for years?" Bishop Jakes responded that it's not that new believers have more faith, but it's because they have no doubt! That was a powerful statement that resonated in my spirit and quickly changed my way of thinking.

Matthew 17:20 references Jesus's teaching that faith the size of a mustard seed will move mountains. Not only will our mustard seed faith move mountains, but we can also tell our mountain to move from here to there, and it shall be done. The fact is, great faith is not required for great results but only faith. Abraham did not waver in unbelief (Romans 4:20), and he received the promise (Hebrews 11:11). However, Abraham tried to birth the promise on his own by impregnating his servant Hagar (Genesis 16:16), yet he *still* received the promise. Though he had challenges in his faith and tried to create his own promise, his latter removal of doubt caused his promise to come to fruition, and he became a biblical example of faith.

Matthew 13:58 outlines the fact that many people who came in direct contact with Jesus, the Savior, saw no miracles because of their lack of faith. I made the decision that I do not want to be like the people who had access to Jesus but never saw manifestations because of unbelief. God reminded me of the book of Mark Chapter 9:19–25, where there was a man who had a son who was possessed by evil spirits for years, and Jesus said to him, "Anything is possible to him who believes."

The man responds to Jesus, "I believe, but help my unbelief," then Jesus casted out the evil spirits. In the midst of unbelief, faith was still present, and that mustard seed, this tiny little seed, produced great results. I've learned not to focus on unbelief and the religious steps and processes but to focus on faith in God and His word. Hebrews 11 contains numerous reference points of those who received the promises of God through faith. These examples yield a new perception of truth that is based on biblical facts and increased my ability to believe and not doubt (Mark 11:23).

To balance the scale, I do believe that discipline and following the principles of God are needed in order to live a faith-filled life. The principles of God are not created to bring people into bondage, but they're created as a preparatory process of learning to manage the liberation and next-level blessings that God has ordained. For example, tithing is not about giving a preacher money, but it's a discipline and a principle that sets the stage for prioritizing finances and budgeting while also advancing kingdom works. Eating healthy food and exercise nurture the body, and they give the necessary strength and energy to complete the works that God has ordained. The principles of God should not be ignored because of faith, but faith should be activated and sustained by those principles. James 2:18 states, "I will show you my faith by my works." Faith is not a program or multistep process for accomplishing God's plan. Faith is the conviction that what I am believing to happen will happen. Because I believe (faith), I'm preparing for it (discipline).

Faith is a powerful component of accepted truths. Once I realized that God is bigger than my mistakes and shortcomings, I began to release my faith and accept the truths of God's word as it concerns me. As I began to change my accepted truth and allow faith to be activated, manifestations of God's blessings began to surface in my life. Living a life of faith and understanding who I am in Christ has been my foundation for satisfaction. It's not tied to a relationship, a job, a title, or a social status, but it's tied to my core of knowing who God has created me to be. It's knowing that God will provide everything I need. It's knowing that God's word is my truth. It's knowing that with long life, God will satisfy me (Psalms 91:16).

The Exit

I learned to adapt to varying seasons and emotions of a single, and I've gained a level of contentment and peace in being alone. It seemed that singleness would be the region I would reside in forever, and I began to settle for the remainder of my life's journey. I began a one-year plan to read the entire Bible, which I had attempted numerous times before but never completed because I became bored and burned out reading through Old Testament laws and regulations, but this time was different.

As I began reading the ordinances that God placed on the children of Israel while they were in the wilderness, I realized that God was training and preparing them for the new season that they were about to enter. He wanted them to be wise and diligent and possess the tenacity to maintain and thrive in the land that He was taking them to. I've heard people say that it took them forty years to cross the street, but I do not believe that it was all due to their negligence in following God. I believe it was God's training camp of preparation to prepare them to not only enter into the promise land but also to have the ability to sustain it. Their frustration in the preparation caused them to give up and negate the promises God had for them. It was frustration that caused Moses to hit the rock with a stick instead of speaking to it as God asked him to do. It was frustration that caused many of the children of Israel to desire their old lifestyle of slavery versus the boot camp of preparation for freedom. It was frustration that caused many of the children of Israel to create gods that they could see versus completing the training camp of preparation that the true and living God was taking them through.

In summary, it was this frustration that caused them to not complete the preparation process, and it cost them their next level blessing. As a single, I often find myself having wilderness experiences of being alone and struggling with the preparation that God takes me through. God showed me that my alone time is preparation for the next level and new dimension of a God-ordained relationship. God brings two people together for a common purpose and kingdom pursuits. He doesn't want to bring people together just so they can sit and watch TV and enjoy another's company at dinner. Instead, He brings them together as a unified force for the kingdom advancement.

The seasons/cycles through singleness is a preparatory training camp for developing a stronger and more intimate relationship with God and self. In order to know how to build a strong, intimate relationship with someone else, I have to first build a strong and intimate relationship with God. God requires to be first place and first priority, and when He gets that place, then He can allow a second place, third place, and so on.

I began to believe that I would be single forever, and I began to accept that reality for my life. But then I heard a still small voice deep inside, and it was God telling me, "I have not called you to be single." I almost felt that was worse than being called to singleness because I know how to live and operate by myself, and I can dissolve any interactions or potential companions along the way. I have not been on a date in over three years and don't even know how or where to begin dating. Nonetheless, God reminded me that His vision is also His provision!

God told Moses to tell the pharaoh (king) at the time to release His people from slavery in Egypt. Moses asked God, "Who do I tell him sent me?" God responded, "Tell him I am that I am has sent you." At that moment, God placed His authority in Moses to become the authority in speaking to the king. However, that wasn't enough for Moses. He asked God to allow Aaron to do the talking because he stuttered, and God granted his request. Aaron and Moses went to the king using Moses's authority and Aaron's voice requesting the release of the children of Israel from slavery. The pharaoh did not let the children of God go without a fight, and God sent plague after plague after plague to convince the king to release the children of Israel. After he finally released them, he thought about what he had done and chased after them. His chase to destroy was literally a chase to his own death as God drowned him and his entire army in the Red Sea.

I've learned that I have often been the pharaoh of my life by hanging on to bondages and struggles that I did not want to release because they were familiar spirits and comfortable defaults. Adapting to disappointments and inconsistencies of love ones and friends caused me to always doubt and to subconsciously wait for the bomb to drop in every relationship. Growing up, I had people who were my friend today and tomorrow act as if they never knew me. There was no argument, no disagreement, no warning, but just a flip of the script. Three or four days later, they treated me as though I was their best friend. My mom never seemed to want to be bothered with me, and she rarely allowed me to go over friends' houses because she said that they didn't want to be bothered with me either. Those comments created a fear that my presence would somehow inconvenience others, and I developed a standoffish behavior because I believed that others really didn't want to be bothered with me. These are a few stones that build the foundation of my personality and the pharaoh of my life for many years. It has taken the hand of God to shift this mindset and to view myself the way that God views me. To be honest, I still wrestle with that pharaoh!

After years of failed relationships, isolation, fear, and building emotional barriers, I was finally able to shift into the emotional space that God has been trying to pull me into for years. Years of experience in the wrong mindset resulted in years of recovery, restoration, and reset of the mind. I've always known that I needed a shift but never knew or understood how to shift. God allowed all my efforts to fail so that I could finally realize that it's not in me to shift, but my shift is in God. I had to stop trying to figure everything out and learn that it's not for me to understand and plan everything for my life. My life was created by God; He's the manufacturer. Consequently, returning myself to the manufacturer for repair is the only way that I will be able to function optimally. I've heard it said that in order to know the purpose of a thing, you can't ask the thing itself. Instead, you must ask the one who made the thing. God is my creator, and I must go to him in order to understand why I was created (purpose). Although I like to plan my way, I had to learn how to step back and allow God to order my steps (Proverbs 16:9). Understanding that I was chosen (1 Peter 2:9) and predestined (Romans 8:29) for this very moment caused an awakening for me to understand the moments around me.

The discomforts, agitations, crisis, and distresses are all part of the preparation process. Frustration is a real challenge for me and is the primary culprit driving me to give up. It's the simple agitations that caused me to move into frustration and out of preparation. It's the discomforts that drive the need to search for comfort versus maintaining focus on the purpose and the vision. It's the crisis and the shifting of normalcy that causes frustration in the pursuit of destiny. God reminded me of the children of Israel's wilderness experience to encourage me not to allow the simplicity of frustration to starve faith and reject destiny. I began to understand why things were happening to me and understood that it wasn't coincidence or happenstance but an intentional growth process and my boot camp for the next level of blessings that God prepared for my life. My husband will show up only when I complete the preparation process and am prepared to not only obtain but also sustain a God-given husband. It is then and only then that I will exit the seasons of singleness and enter into the seasons of marriage.

Conclusion

Singleness is more than a season but rather a region of continual shifting of seasons that effect mental, emotional, and spiritual well-being. It is critical to prepare for these fluctuating seasons in advance. Singleness is not a sign of failure or necessarily unrealistic relationship expectations, but it's a visible monument of God's grace, which is always sufficient! God has graced me for the region of singleness! Just as I didn't desire to move across country from a warm climate to a cold climate, I did not desire to reside in the region of singleness. However, the move was truly a blessing, and I was able to grow in all areas of my life. The same is true for my time of singleness. This time has truly been a blessing and has allowed me to grow in all areas of my life. I am learning more about who I am and am still discovering the world around me. God has orchestrated every step of my life, including my seasons of singleness.

Life is like a coin. I can spend it any way I want, but I can only spend it once. So I try to live it to the fullest till it overflows (John 10:10 AMP). My joyous life is not contingent upon another person, but it is contingent upon yielding to the complete plan of God, which yields a satisfaction and joy that cannot be duplicated or found in anyone else. While God's preparing me, he's also preparing my spouse, and one day, my divine connection will occur, and my lifelong partner will be with me as we both fulfill our God-given purposes and reach our God-given destinies.

A Single's Prayer

Lord, I thank you for your grace and mercy and for being the wonderful and mighty God that you are. I ask God that you search my heart and mind and remove anything that is not like you. I ask God that you shelter my heart from harmful intents and that you renew my mind to make godly and biblical decisions in every area of my life. Help me to respect and appreciate the grace that you've given me to live as a godly single and help me to give you honor in everything that I do. I ask that you give me a keen sense of discernment to recognize every plot and trick that the enemy has set before me. Help me to recognize and cling to the godly relationships that you have ordained in my life and abhor any toxic relationships.

I rebuke spirits of fear, doubt, and unbelief, and I release faith and expectancy in every area of my life. Help me to wait for a spouse with patience knowing that you are an intentional God who has intentionally placed me where I am today. I am loved, I am attractive, I am not alone, and I am successful. No weapon formed against my mind, my thoughts, my intellect, my self-esteem, my self-worth, my value, my well-being, or my body shall prosper. I am a child of the most-high God, a royal priesthood, and no good thing will you withhold from me because I walk upright. I am the righteousness of God, and I am blessed and highly favored. I will walk in joy and peace and will receive everything that you have prepared for me.

In Jesus's name, amen.

About the Author

Rhunda Armstead, a native of Mississippi by way of Indiana, currently resides in the greater Nashville area and has worked in corporate America in roles ranging from software developer to business analyst in the health-care industry. Rhunda has an undergraduate degree in computer information systems, a master's degree in business administration, and a graduate certification in health informatics. Rhunda has been a Christian since age fifteen and has served in many capacities in church ministry since her teenage years.

Having over twenty years of experience as a Christian single, Rhunda learned how to navigate emotional gaps in her life that were not always fulfilled through professional achievements, serving in ministry, or relationships. With God's direction and His leading through the Holy Spirit, she has obtained wisdom and discipline to maintain a life of morale, principle, and peace. She has been able to apply biblical principles to everyday life in a manner that has allowed her to not compromise her faith while maintaining peace and joy in the Lord. These biblical applications and experiences are shared in this book, *Seasons of Singleness*.

References

https://www.census.gov/topics/families/families-and-households.html.

https://www.psychologytoday.com/us/blog/living-single/201908/around-the-world-marriage-is-declining-singles-are-rising.

https://www.washingtonpost.com/news/soloish/wp/2016/09/20/what-has-changed-for-single-americans-in-the-past-decade/?noredirect=on.

https://www.psychologytoday.com/us/blog/living-single/201810/the-rise-single-people-why-some-find-it-scary.

https://en.wikipedia.org/wiki/Oymyakon.

https://www.wired.com/2015/01/amos-chapple-the-coldest-place-on-earth/.

https://www.bbc.com/news/world-11875131.

https://www.coastalhomeplans.com/ten-tips-building-coast/.

Notes

Notes

Notes

_____
_____
_____
_____
_____
_____
_____
_____
_____
_____
_____
_____
_____
_____
_____
_____
_____
_____
_____
_____
_____
_____
_____
_____
_____

Printed in the USA
CPSIA information can be obtained
at www.ICGtesting.com
LVHW091805100224
771306LV00004B/772